Pebble™

Weather

Ice

by Helen Frost

Consulting Editor: Gail Saunders-Smith, Ph.D.
Consultant: Joseph M. Moran, Ph.D., Meteorologist
Associate Director, Education Program
American Meteorological Society

Pebble Books are published by Capstone Press
151 Good Counsel Drive, P.O. Box 669, Mankato, Minnesota 56002
www.capstonepress.com

1 2 3 4 5 6 09 08 07 06 05 04

Library of Congress Cataloging-in-Publication Data
Frost, Helen, 1949–
    Ice / by Helen Frost.
        p. cm.—(Weather)
    Summary: Simple text and photographs present ice, how it is formed, and how
it affects the Earth and people.
    Includes bibliographical references and index.
    ISBN 0-7368-2094-9 (hardcover)
    1. Ice—Juvenile literature. [1. Ice.] I. Title. II. Series: Weather (Mankato, Minn.)
QC926.37.F73 2004
551.34—dc22   2003013405

Note to Parents and Teachers

The Weather series supports national science standards related
to earth science. This book describes and illustrates ice. The
photographs support early readers in understanding the text. The
repetition of words and phrases helps early readers learn new
words. This book also introduces early readers to subject-specific
vocabulary words, which are defined in the Glossary. Early readers
may need assistance to read some words and to use the Table of
Contents, Glossary, Read More, Internet Sites, and Index/Word List
sections of the book.

Table of Contents

What Is Ice?

Ice is frozen water. It is cold and slippery. Water can be a solid, a liquid, or a gas. Ice is water as a solid.

Water freezes at 32 degrees Fahrenheit (0 degrees Celsius). Ice melts at higher temperatures.

8

Ice makes sidewalks and roads slippery. People put sand or salt on icy roads and sidewalks to make them safer.

10

Types of Ice

Rain sometimes freezes when it hits something cold. Freezing rain covers roads, trees, and wires. The weight of the ice can break tree branches.

Sleet is many small pieces of ice. Sleet begins as snowflakes. The snowflakes melt and then freeze again into ice as they fall to the ground.

Hail forms in thunderstorm clouds. Hailstones are balls of ice. They can be smaller than peas or bigger than golf balls.

Rivers and Lakes

Rivers and lakes freeze when the temperature stays cold. The water at the top freezes first.

People can fish or skate
when ice is thick. But it is
not safe to walk on thin ice.
People can fall through thin
ice into the cold water.

Melting

Ice melts into water. The water soaks into the ground or flows into rivers and lakes. Ice on rivers breaks into chunks, floats away, and melts.

Glossary

freeze—to become solid at a low temperature; water freezes at 32 degrees Fahrenheit (0 degrees Celsius).

freezing rain—raindrops that freeze when they hit something cold

hail—small balls of ice that form in thunderstorm clouds; hail falls from the sky; the balls of ice are called hailstones when they hit the ground.

ice—frozen water; water can be a solid, a liquid, or a gas; ice is a solid.

liquid—a wet substance that can be poured

melt—to change from a solid to a liquid; ice melts above 32 degrees Fahrenheit (0 degrees Celsius).

sleet—small ice pieces formed when melted snowflakes refreeze before reaching the ground

solid—something that holds its shape; a solid is not a liquid or a gas; ice is water as a solid.

Read More

Bundey, Nikki. *Ice and the Earth.* The Science of Weather. Minneapolis: Carolrhoda, 2001.

Frost, Helen. *Water as a Solid.* Water. Mankato, Minn.: Pebble Books, 2000.

Pipe, Jim. *Why Does Ice Melt?* How? What? Why? Brookfield, Conn.: Copper Beech Books, 2002.

Internet Sites

FactHound offers a safe, fun way to find Internet sites related to this book. All of the sites on FactHound have been researched by our staff.

Here's how:

1. Visit *www.facthound.com*

2. Type in this special code **0736820949** for age-appropriate sites. Or enter a search word related to this book for a more general search.

3. Click on the **Fetch It** button.

FactHound will fetch the best sites for you!

Index/Word List

break, 11
cold, 5, 11, 17, 19
freeze, 7, 11, 13, 17
freezing rain, 11
frozen, 5
ground, 13, 21
hail, 15
lakes, 17, 21
melt, 7, 13, 21
rivers, 17, 21
roads, 9, 11

salt, 9
sand, 9
sidewalks, 9
skate, 19
sleet, 13
slippery, 5, 9
snowflakes, 13
solid, 5
temperature, 7, 17
thunderstorm, 15
water, 5, 7, 17, 19, 21

Word Count: 201
Early-Intervention Level: 18

Editorial Credits
Martha E. H. Rustad, editor; Timothy Halldin, series designer; Molly Nei, book
    designer; Deirdre Barton, photo researcher; Karen Risch, product planning editor

Photo Credits
Brand X Pictures/Bob Rashid, 1; Corbis/Craig Tuttle, 20; Corbis/Gary W. Carter, 10;
Corbis/Layne Kennedy, 14, 18; Corbis/Richard Cummins, cover; Steve Mulligan, 16;
Unicorn Stock Photos/Aneal V. Vohra, 8; Unicorn Stock Photos/Jeff Greenberg, 12;
Unicorn Stock Photos/Joel Dexter, 4; Unicorn Stock Photos/Ted Rose, 6

The author thanks the children's library staff at the Allen County Public Library in
Fort Wayne, Indiana, for research assistance.